AQ130

Bright
Ideas

Text: Sharon Dalgleish

Consultant: Richard Wood, Curator, Powerhouse Museum, Sydney

This edition first published 2003 by

MASON CREST PUBLISHERS INC.

370 Reed Road

Broomall, PA 19008

© Weldon Owen Inc.

Conceived and produced by

Weldon Owen Pty Limited

Library of Congress Cataloging-in-Publication Data
on file at the Library of Congress
ISBN: 1-59084-162-X

Printed in Singapore.

1 2 3 4 5 6 7 8 9 06 05 04 03

CONTENTS

EVERYDAY HELPERS

We use some things so often that it's hard to imagine a time when we didn't have them. Many of these inventions didn't work well the first time they were made, but the inventors kept trying new ideas and materials until they got it right.

Umbrella
The umbrella was used in ancient China to give shade from the sun, not shelter from the rain.

Matches
The first matches were not safe. They could light on their own.

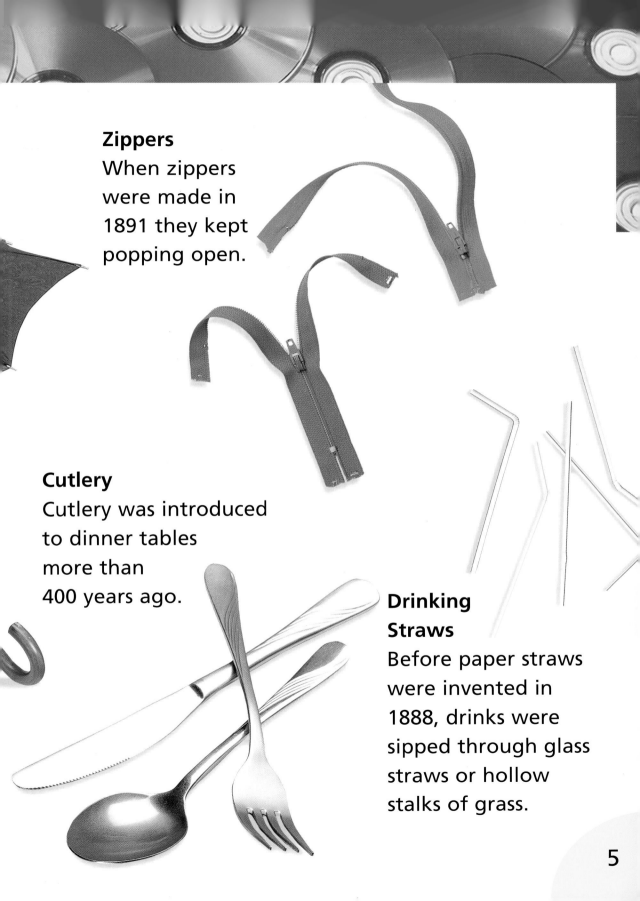

Zippers

When zippers were made in 1891 they kept popping open.

Cutlery

Cutlery was introduced to dinner tables more than 400 years ago.

Drinking Straws

Before paper straws were invented in 1888, drinks were sipped through glass straws or hollow stalks of grass.

Some inventions make our lives easier. Some make our lives safer. Some help us to do things faster. Some are just meant to be fun. All these everyday things were once new and exciting inventions.

Rake
The first rakes were made of wood more than 1,400 years ago.

Escalator
Escalators were invented in 1894 as rides in an amusement park.

Electric Drill

The modern electric drill is a lot lighter than the hand drill invented in 1917—it weighed 24 pounds!

Barbed Wire

The inventor of barbed wire got the idea from plants with thorns.

Traffic Light

Unlike traffic lights today, the first traffic light had only a red light—the signal to stop.

7

AT SCHOOL

Inventions are often simple ways of solving simple problems. It's hard to imagine how we would do our schoolwork without these small but clever items.

Pencils
Graphite has been used for writing for more than 400 years.

Sticky Notes
These were invented in 1980 by a scientist who wanted to mark his place in his hymn book.

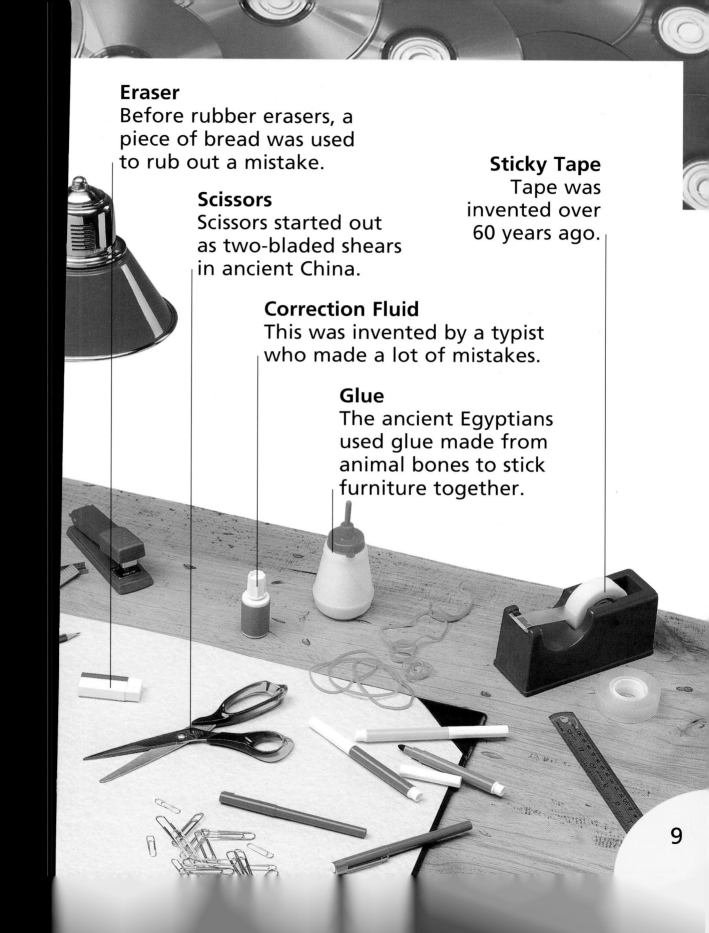

Eraser
Before rubber erasers, a piece of bread was used to rub out a mistake.

Scissors
Scissors started out as two-bladed shears in ancient China.

Sticky Tape
Tape was invented over 60 years ago.

Correction Fluid
This was invented by a typist who made a lot of mistakes.

Glue
The ancient Egyptians used glue made from animal bones to stick furniture together.

9

DID YOU KNOW?

This bicycle invented in 1790 was called a dandy horse. It was pushed along with the feet.

Trunk at Front
The original Beetle is different from other cars. Its engine is at the back.

GETTING AROUND

The first car was invented in 1769. It had three wheels and ran on steam. You could have overtaken it by walking quickly! Early cars were made by hand and were expensive. But by the time the first Volkswagen Beetle hit the road in 1936, millions of people could afford to buy and drive a car.

Windshield Wipers
The first windshield wipers were turned by hand!

Seat Belts
These life-savers were invented nearly 100 years ago, but not widely used until the 1970s.

Brakes
The brakes push against the inside of the wheel to stop it from turning.

Air-filled Rubber Tires
These were invented more than 100 years ago.

PLAYTIME

People have always invented ways to have fun. Some games are fads that are popular one day and gone the next. Other games have been around for hundreds of years and are still played today.

Marbles
The ancient Romans played games of marbles more than 2,000 years ago.

Chess
Chess was invented in India about 1,500 years ago.

Playing Cards

Playing cards, together with special picture cards, were used for fortune-telling in the 1300s.

STRANGE BUT TRUE

In 1845, in Connecticut, a new law banned nine-pin bowling. That didn't stop the bowlers. They added a tenth pin and kept bowling.

Lego

Lego bricks were made in 1949. Two eight-studded bricks can be joined in 24 different ways. Try it!

Space Shuttle

A shuttle is a spaceship that can be used again. The crew on board launches new satellites and fixes those that are broken.

Astronaut

To fly through space, astronauts use an invention that looks like a rocket-powered chair.

INTO SPACE

Space is a dangerous place. Many of the materials we use every day were invented for use there. Some bicycles are now made of the same material used to build light and strong spaceships. Sunglasses that were specially designed to reduce glare in space are now worn on Earth.

Space Station
A space station is home
for astronauts working
in space.

Satellites
Satellites
orbit the
Earth to send
back weather information
and TV and radio signals.

15

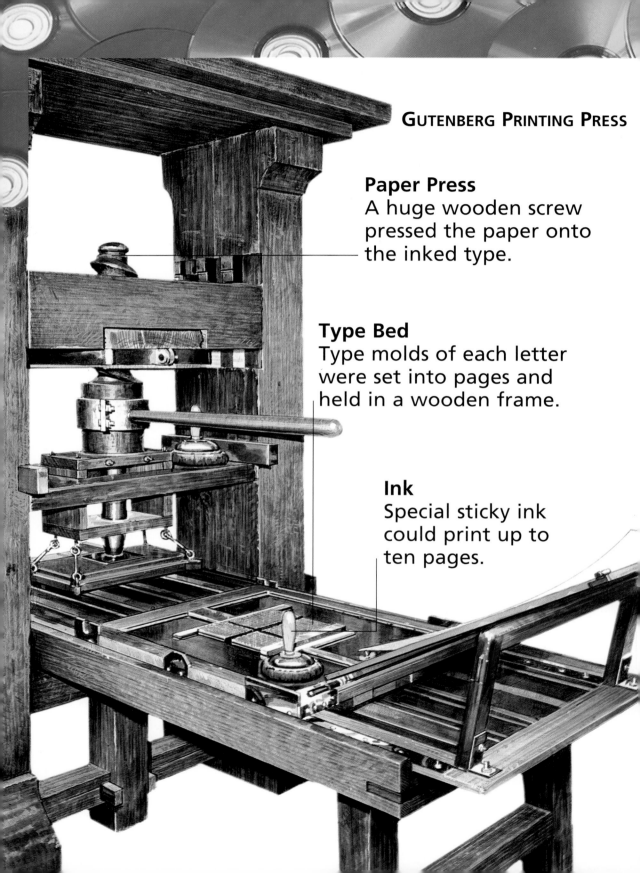

GUTENBERG PRINTING PRESS

Paper Press
A huge wooden screw pressed the paper onto the inked type.

Type Bed
Type molds of each letter were set into pages and held in a wooden frame.

Ink
Special sticky ink could print up to ten pages.

PRINTING

Inventions help us to communicate in different ways. One of the most important inventions was the printing press made by Johannes Gutenberg in 1447. It had metal molds to print each letter. These molds could be used again. They were moved around to make the words on the different pages.

DID YOU KNOW?

Braille is writing made up of raised dots in soft paper. It was invented so blind people could read by touch.

Paper Bed
This held the printed paper while it dried.

TELEPHONE

In the 1830s the telegraph was invented. It sent a code of beeps along wires over long distances. The code had to be sorted back into words at the other end. Then, in 1876, Alexander Graham Bell invented the telephone. Now the human voice could be sent along a wire and heard at the other end.

CANDLESTICK PHONE

This is what early telephones looked like. How do you answer the telephone? Alexander Graham Bell thought they should be answered by saying, "Hoy, hoy!"

Telephone Exchange
Operators had to join telephone wires so people could talk to each other.

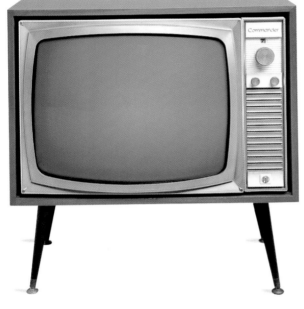

Headphones
These are based on hearing aids invented in 1901.

Television
In 1923 John Logie Baird started putting together a lot of inventions by other people to make a mechanical television.

MUSIC AND PICTURES

Have you ever made shadow puppets? That's how people told stories on cave walls. They used shells and bones to make music. The first projector was invented in 1640. It was called a magic lantern. Now we have television, film, radio, and computers to bring us pictures and music.

Saxophone

Adolphe Sax invented the saxophone in 1841. He practiced for 11 years before he taught others to play.

Guitar

A type of guitar was played in the Middle East as early as 3,000 years ago.

Compact Discs

The CD was invented in 1981. Sound is recorded as tiny changes to the surface of the plastic.

AT THE DOCTOR

Going to the doctor two hundred years ago was very different from today. Patients were awake and had to be tied down during operations! In 1846 doctors started using a chemical called ether to make a patient fall asleep during the operation.

STETHOSCOPE

A stethoscope listens to sounds inside the body. It makes them louder and passes them through tubes into earpieces. When it was invented in 1816, it had only one earpiece.

CLOCKS

Before clocks were invented, people used the sun to tell the time. The ancient Egyptians made a water clock. It was like a bucket with a hole near the bottom. By the 1600s there were clocks with cogs and wheels. Inventors used similar gears to make early calculators. Those calculators led to the computers we use today.

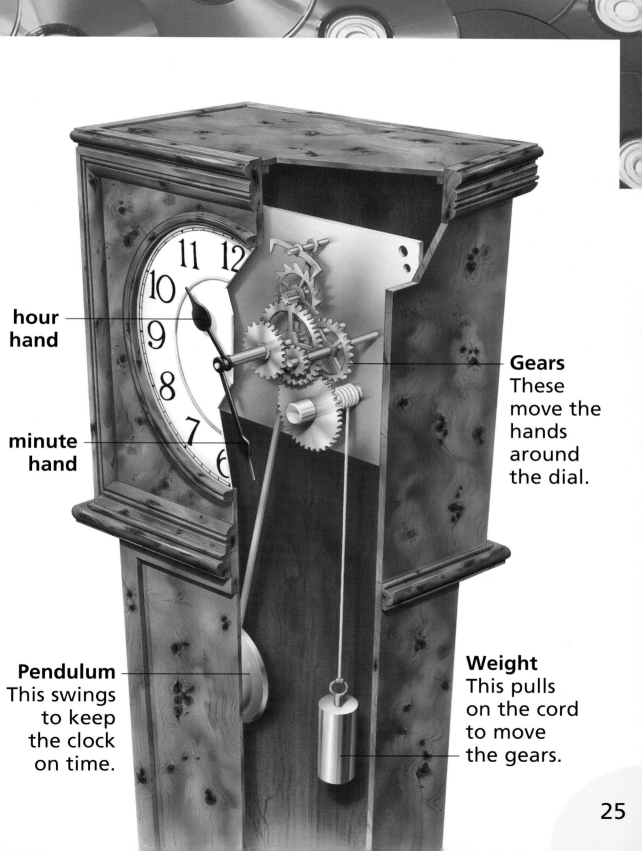

hour hand

minute hand

Gears
These move the hands around the dial.

Pendulum
This swings to keep the clock on time.

Weight
This pulls on the cord to move the gears.

25

EARLY POWER

Steam power was first used in ancient Alexandria (in Egypt) to spin a ball. People thought it was just a toy. It was not until the 1600s that inventors started using it again. Soon steam was used to power engines to pump water, run factories, move ships, and even drive merry-go-rounds. Steam is still used today. Most electricity is still made using huge steam-driven generators.

AMAZING!

The electric iron was invented in 1882. But nobody wanted one because most houses didn't have electricity connected!

DID YOU KNOW?

In the 1500s, knights wore chain mail and heavy metal armor. Today, butchers wear chain mail gloves to protect their hands.

Battle Armor

Over five hundred years ago the inventor and artist Leonardo da Vinci drew terrible fighting machines. They were protected by metal armor and could travel over muddy fields. In 1916 the tank was invented and used in World War I. This modern United Nations tank has a lookout post.

Armor Plating
This is now made of light but strong metals, plastics, and even ceramics.

Caterpillar Tracks
The track belt under the wheels helps the tank cross any ground in any weather.

GLOSSARY

calculator A machine that can add, subtract, multiply, and divide numbers.

cog A notch or tooth on a wheel.

gears Wheels with teeth that turn other wheels.

graphite A soft form of carbon used in pencils.

invention An original or new product or process.

orbit To spin in a circular pattern around a planet, the way a satellite spins around the Earth.

projector A machine that shines a large image onto a screen.

type In the printing industry, a rectangular piece of metal with a raised letter on one side.

Index

PICTURE AND ILLUSTRATION CREDITS

BOOKS IN THIS SERIES

WEIRD AND WONDERFUL WILDLIFE	LAND, SEA, AND SKY	INFORMATION STATION
Incredible Creatures	Sharks and Rays	Every Body Tells a Story
Creepy Creatures	Underwater Animals	The Human Body
Scaly Things	Mammals of the Sea	**Bright Ideas**
Feathers and Flight	Ocean Life	Out and About
Attack and Defense	Volcanoes	Exploring Space
Snakes	Weather Watching	High Flying
Hidden World	Maps and Our World	How Things Work
Reptiles and Amphibians	Earthquakes	Native Americans
Mini Mammals	The Plant Kingdom	Travelers and Traders
Up and Away	Rain or Shine	Sports for All
Mighty Mammals	Sky Watch	People from the Past
Dangerous Animals	The Planets	Play Ball!